Evenings on Paisley Avenue
Seven Hamilton Poets

Evenings on Paisley Avenue
Seven Hamilton Poets

Editor
Marilyn Gear Pilling

Marilyn Gear Pilling

First Edition

Hidden Brook Press
www.HiddenBrookPress.com
writers@HiddenBrookPress.com

Evenings on Paisley Avenue: Seven Hamilton Poets
Editor – Marilyn Gear Pilling
Authors – Pauline Hewak
– Paddy Chitty
– Kimberley Dawn
– Birgit Elston
– Laura Gillis
– Sandra Lloyd
– Elizabeth Tessier

Cover Photograph – Dan Pilling
Cover Design – Richard M. Grove
Layout and Design – Richard M. Grove

Typeset in Garamond
Printed and bound in USA

Library and Archives Canada Cataloguing in Publication

Evenings on Paisley Avenue : seven Hamilton poets / editor, Marilyn Gear Pilling.

ISBN 978-1-927725-09-2 (pbk.)

1. Canadian poetry (English)--Ontario--Hamilton. 2. Canadian poetry (English)--21st century. I. Pilling, Marilyn Gear, 1945-, editor

PS8295.7.H34E94 2014 C811'.6080971352 C2014-902228-X

This book is dedicated to Hamilton,
to its thriving writing community,
and to
Bryan Prince Bookseller.

Contents

Birgit Elston

Laura Gillis

Sandra Lloyd

Elizabeth Tessier

Introduction by the Editor Marilyn Gear Pilling

I met the seven poets featured in this book when they were my students in McMaster University's Creative Writing Certificate Program. A couple of years after McMaster discontinued this program, the group approached me to continue to teach them privately from home. So began our Evenings on Paisley Avenue.

We have worked together for years now, and in the winter of 2013, a publisher happened to be in the audience when Pauline Hewak read her poetry aloud as an opening reader for the Hamilton Poetry Centre. While the audience mingled after the reading, the publisher approached Pauline and me, and said that he would like to publish Pauline's work as a book, if I would edit it. Pauline had not written enough poems for a book. A couple of weeks later, I let the publisher know that we had a group of seven equally-talented poets, and proposed that he publish a selection of work by all seven. He agreed.

To have a book fall into one's lap like this, in these days, is as rare as sighting a three-toed sloth having coffee in Westdale Village. I am delighted to introduce readers to each of these seven talented Hamilton and area writers, all of whom are now being published, poem by poem, in a wide variety of journals.

Pauline Hewak

Hamilton has inspired the first five poems of Pauline Hewak's selection. "Under the Escarpment" is a fast ride through the narrator's ninth summer. The language puts us there *barefoot wild / those fat summers*, the run-on lines pull us through, details pop off the page: *the hot night stuck to our pyjamas*. "Remembering Then" takes us back to a childhood experience of illness; uneaten rice pudding sits *on the silent ivory celluloid radio / my father had found*, and the worried family is almost as silent as the radio.

"The Sisters of Notre Dame on Snake Road" takes as its jumping off point the *drying racks* bought by an adult narrator *at auction when they / tore the place down.* The narrator makes surprising use of the racks: *I…hung / my sins on them.* "25 Charlton" evokes the universal experience of the medical waiting room and *sitting on the edge of the bed / at two in the morning.* "After the Corktown" mixes winter with beer and doomed love.

Hewak's is a questing, restless sensibility that is capable of producing both images that haunt – a woman as *an unnamed planet* turning in her sky, the house as *a crypt for bad decisions* and images that sing with lyricism—*sunlight spread like doilies upon pine needles.* This poet can surprise you, tossing off a little piece with a country twang—*all my roads to love / chained closed / broken down highway / lines fading into bush / leaving me like / road kill... / and no motel / 'til Wawa,* and taking you back to ancient Sicily, *blood running over the marble altar.*

One thing is constant. Hewak's mercurial narrators range both near and far, and always have the power to sweep us into their worlds.

Paddy Chitty

From this poet's work, I've selected the poems that have their feet in the history of Hamilton, Ontario. The notorious Evelyn Dick—*an ancient woman…backlit by blue / lights*; the watering holes of the 1960's where the *lounges were two-faced—men only, and ladies & escorts*; proms at Memorial Public School—*Dance partners / size each other up like adversaries / in High Noon*; TV pictures that *rolled. Flurries to blizzard to wobbly / diagonal bands*; the boathouse colony that looked like *stranded snipe on the western shore* and were looked down on by the city elite *who'd spat their scorn onto the sheets of the Hamilton Herald.*

The poems live by their details and their people. The dry cleaner who works under an *umbrella of lethal fumes*, the dry cleaner's daughter her *loose hair whipped-wild, fragrant with Prell,* the invisible mender, how he would pick *threads from hidden hem or seam, / weave, first warp then weft.*

Chitty works with the textures and the fabrics of real life, the feel and the sights, the smells and tastes of lived experience. Her eye misses nothing and her poetic imagination is steeped in history. Her images put us back *there—the turnip and cod caught / in the fabric of her clothing and hair*; the grandfather *stiff as the stilts that moored the boathouse shacks*; the elderly lawyers picking *sweet lamb from the rack of past trials.* These poems jolt our memories and by implication make startling comparisons between then and now.

Kimberley Dawn

An almost mystical identification with nature and an appreciation of the beauty and the healing power of landscape (*the silence / that soothes the edge / of August*) are the most dominant characteristics of the work of this poet. *Slipping into the deep / gilt lake* is where we are most likely to find the narrators of Dawn's poems – *alone between / sun and moon / and dragonfly-hover.*

Even when her narrators are in the city, they are most likely to be found out of doors, aware of and in tune with what surrounds them. At times, this identification with nature seems almost to amount to a religion. From "On Sunday": *Meditative laps at Victoria Park a part / of my liturgy.*

In Dawn's "Where to Meet Men," Hamilton stars again. The narrator is on a trek up Locke Street past *trendy shops*, and among *texters, buggy-pushers and kale- / lovers.* She is on her way to the 330 steps and *an unmatched / view of the city, the Bay and beyond.* This poem demonstrates another characteristic of Dawn's poetry – a tolerance of the other, a willingness to engage with the stranger, an open-hearted readiness to join in with the rituals and customs of others. From "On Sundays": *The man hugs and blesses / Joshua and his brother into the fold / and I slip into holy water.*

Follow this poet through the ten poems of her days and ways. Then walk where she walks. You might be lucky enough to find a Kimberley Dawn poem clinging to the escarpment, sitting on a lily pad or tucked into the knothole of a tree.

Birgit Elston

This is the work of a poet who is from a city built on water and this element has formed her poetic imagination. Water—subtlety, fluidity, impermanence, depths that may flow into death. Elston's imagination moves with the fluidity of water and her writing is replete with images of impermanence: *evening melts / on my tongue; a fleeting quadrangle of light in blue snow; the empty seat between us; drops of vapour / gliding along the washing line; the thinning sounds / of people and cars taking leave.*

The feet of these poems are not quite on the ground. You have the feeling that any one of them could metamorphose into another form at any time, like the husband who suddenly turns into an old man in a nursing home, looking with wonder at the deer, or the old man whose life of work and Friday drives to the lake has evaporated so completely that it seems to have been another's life. There is a fey element to Elston's work, a feeling that the invisible world hovers close. There are presences that haunt, a sadness. Though there may be a longing for *careless summer adventures*, this is essentially a poetry of cold, blue snow, *frail sun*, icicles, *silver-striped* water, early darkness, a poetry where the silence speaks as eloquently as the words, and there is always the possibility that the wolf may break free of his shackles.

Laura Gillis

What drives the work of this poet is conflict. The beating heart of each poem is the tension experienced by the narrator between two different worlds. In "Buffet," for instance, one world is represented by the *all you can eat…mounds and towers* of mass-produced food, the other by the family dinner—food that carries meaning (sweet and bitter), the expected visitation from the non-material, discarnate world (*as we opened the door / to ask the prophet Elijah to come to us.*) "Buffet" is a good demonstration of Gillis's way of working. One world is set beside the other without comment. The vivid details speak for themselves. They sing and sizzle. They blossom and cut to the bone. The reader makes the connections.

Intensity and a determination to be honest—these are the qualities that characterize the voice of these poems. Yet, beneath is an almost-hidden vulnerability. And the speaker's direct gaze spares no one, least of all herself: "I have ugly things going on."

These poems pull at the heart. A longing for the elements of life that transcend the purely material values of the *affluent suburb / surrounded by big box stores* is palpable. It infuses and drives the work. It leaves the reader with a clearer vision of the soullessness of our North American culture and touches down on those moments that hold so much more: *My aunt cried quietly beside me / then leaned over and smiled, / wiped a strand of hair from my eyes.*

Sandra Lloyd

A background in science and an exploring intelligence have led this poet to write about subjects as disparate as the complicated relationships human beings may have with trees, the characteristics of a meromictic lake and the custom of dumping outhouse pails in the street. Her subject may even be language itself: *I lie / like sweet treasure, awakening / to the fact that it's pointless / to be immersed here / in a dead language.*

The sensibility evident in this work is feeling balanced by thinking. The writer's narrative personas are as various as a tourist on a St. Maarten beach, a student dreaming about a professor, and the voice of "Surface Tension" which I would characterize as having a dispassionate surface and a melancholic underbelly. The tone of Lloyd's work ranges from the humorous telling of "Displacement in Westdale Village" to the lyrical intimacy of "Subjunctive Moods" to the crystalline strangeness of "Crawford Lake."

Lloyd achieves her effects at times through form, as in "Displacement," where the run-on lines create the tone which is the basis of the subtle humour. Repetition is a crucial element of "Subjunctive Moods," where the repeated long sigh of the *Uhta*, followed by *the breathing space for wishful thinking*, serves both as a jumping off place for the poet's meditation and a motif that provides a resting place for the reader. Or the effect may come by means of a light touch that leaves as much unsaid as said and thereby vivifies the reader's interest and imagination, as in "Patternicity."

In other words, it is not easy to characterize the poetry of Sandra Lloyd as a whole; the trajectory of her work, so far, is as mysterious as the three backlit, elegant ruminants she leaves us with: *Cream-coloured roses hang[ing] / from their mouths.*

Elizabeth Tessier

The pervasive features of Elizabeth Tessier's work are these. A cherishing of what has come before—our personal pasts, the stories of the objects that have come down to us, the practices of our ancestors, the mythology and religion and rituals that formed our predecessors' world view. A keen awareness of how what has come before lives on in us. A sense of the connectedness of all things. The mind of her narrators is always in search of meaning and context—from their examination of domestic details to their take on a fundamental text in the Western canon.

Thus, an antique chair in the narrator's bedroom comes from a time when such an investment *might be a sign of hard work / and God's obvious favour*, the custom of preserving is described as *Land of forward planning, / of quiet women boiling up jars / to push through fruitless Februaries.* The angel on the Christmas tree is not just an angel. She represents a *commitment to what feels true / in our religiously irreligious home, / holding to the mysteries of light and birth / without the usual answers.*

The poem "Homecoming" deserves a word of its own. We humans may desire adventure. We also long for stability, a home, a soul mate. "Homecoming" penetrates to the essence of this archetypal theme.

Tessier's poetry is not without humour. But her most characteristic gaze holds a reverence and a thoughtfulness. Her work is deeply soulful, always meaningful.

Pauline Hewak

For Kerry
Thank you so much for your help with all of this! And – thanks for being part of the fun :)
Pauline xxx

Under the Escarpment

We ran barefoot wild
those fat summers the sun
buzzed down on four-square lawns
and sleeping babies in front-porch prams
lulled by the rhythm
of the knife-sharpener's bell.

My father (when business was slow),
made vague plans for a bomb-shelter beside the kiddie-pool
and my mother did another load of pregnancy
waddled through a landscape of laundry
while breast-feeding babies
to the ebb and flow of sirens along Main Street
and the clink of milk bottles set down on the step

and the hot night stuck to our pyjamas.

Pockets full of sunflower seeds, we spat black
hulls on sidewalks and in flower beds
smeared dandelion on sweaty necks
visibly anointed like Ash Wednesday.

Rag-tag packs of neighbourhood boys scoffed penny candy
from Sher-Main Variety
for girls in midriff tops and white runners,
who unwrapped rolls of sour candies with plastic fingernails,
posed with wax lips
birthstone rings
candy cigarettes
pretty pink ash flashing like guns at noon at the O.K. Corral,
doled out coloured powders that turned into liquid jewels
when you spat in the palm of your hand

our teeth black from licorice pipes
we smiled at the swag.

If you shot stones against the cinder-block wall
in the alley behind the store, the stones smelled like gas
hot and industrial and good
like cars and steel mills and jobs.

If you looked between the Cumberland Avenue rail tracks
you could find Lake Iroquois fossils to line up on your window sill
or shake around in a Christmas cookie tin:
a trilobite tambourine.

If you were brave, and a boy, you could climb the roof of St. Peter's Anglican,
perch like a gargoyle
legs dangling, waiting for the street lights
like the boy with the silver front tooth
who climbed alone after supper
got stuck in a hole and shot
baseball cards up and over.

His mother in hair-net and taped-down kiss curls yelled
to wipe that smile off his face
as he waved to the crowd from the fireman's ladder, silver
tooth a star in the gloaming;
she addressed him by his first-day-of-school name
that everyone had forgotten
in the long days and nights of my ninth
summer.

The Sisters of Notre Dame on Snake Road

once hung their stockings on drying racks.
I bought those racks at auction when they
tore the place down.
They went cheap.
I brought them home and hung
my sins on them, at night, in the basement
one by one.

There were iron beds too, rows and rows
of narrow white beds on the grass,
an open-air infirmary, ticking mattresses
exposed, nobody looking.

I set up a bed on my screened
porch, watched bugs crawl,
felt the eyes of small animals as I slept.

Two men paid by the hour
pulled a cupboard out of the convent
wall, one side pine, the other oak,
lugged it up my verandah. I built a new wall
around it, and when I looked
in the grated pass-through
between the two rooms
where the kitchen women once served
meals, unseen,
I saw myself
as I used to be, watching
from my bedroom window, a Salvation Army
tuba glinting under the street lamp.

Remembering Then

People whispered. My aunt brought me
a Mennonite quilt all the way from Kitchener.
They tucked it around me
where I lay, as if to bolster the blood
by the laying on of hands. At night, my fingers
picked at the pattern—pale green
flower baskets and ribbons,
A nurse came to the house to take blood
and when I heard the front door shut, I grew
fearful, her departure signalling
a warning, I thought. The rice pudding
my mother made for me
sat uneaten on the silent ivory celluloid radio
my father had found.
The rash, the swollen eyes, the night sweats
(in the pink night gown sewn sevenfold
for the granddaughters) silenced everyone
and I became accustomed to the whispers.

One morning, the spring spat me out. I landed
barefoot in the garden and my mother
ironed the plaid dress with the heart-shaped
pocket she'd cut out on the dining room table
from a tissue-pattern
when she couldn't sleep.

25 Charlton

You put on your game face because you've read
that your face can make your emotions.
You sit there waiting with the others
looking down at boots
undone, laces salt-stiffened.

Nobody had done up their boots.

We wait
to give up bodily fluids to a haruspex in a lab coat,
respectfully,
because you know that whatever the blood says
you must listen
and that makes you respectful of the needle too
glinting and quick like a shark,
and you are proud of the gush into the test tube and
another set aside for divination,
the meaning
of which you measure
sitting on the edge of the bed
at two in the morning.

After the Corktown

Feeling the sounds
of your words in my mouth
that wisp up cold
in cars on dark nights blue
with ice and longing
or left still warm on beer glass rims
the frozen lines of lips
under streetlight nimbus
I hold onto your edges holding
out against wind
that files me down
and makes the mean streets moan

The End of Winter

I carry sticks home in a plastic bag.
The winter was unrelenting this year.
Why let the street cleaner
sweep away the sticks when they can
keep the fire going?
The house feels like a crypt for bad decisions.

Winter's refuse is smashed in gutters.
Twigs and leaves cleave to pieces of plastic.
Flowers frozen in situ wait—
unworn corsages from last autumn's solstice party
I was too tired to attend.

The lady up the street is dying and every
tree on the street knows it.
A man brushes away leaves
for the snowdrops.
He raises his head to read
my face.

Joe's Cabin

When you said that in the spring it rains inside your cabin,
the wood stove drawing out winter,
I thought you were a conjurer
commanding nature and I wanted you to make me
into a smooth stone for your pocket.

When you said that you invented a colour that disappears at dusk
I wanted to keep you for myself
put you under my tongue like an agate marble, douse
the campfire flames, deny knowledge
of your whereabouts.

When you had me walk behind you, step in your footsteps,
the wind pushing and the snow
drifted two feet deep,
I pressed my forehead into your back,
your back like the Escarpment, intractable and sure.

When we fell away from one another, I stopped thinking about
your cabin, the parts of me that had yielded
to the murmur of trees and your mouth
and sunlight spread like doilies upon pine needles and I forgot
the night sounds lush under a blanket knit of words

like colours warm against the chill of winds pulling across farmland
and we listened to the sound of branches snapping
under the weight of our contentment.

Altar of Hiero

It looks like another innocuous Greek ruin, important
to somebody but not to me, until
the tour guide explains that 450 bulls
were sacrificed simultaneously
blood running over the marble altar
spilling onto soil, soaking the hems of tunics,
sandals, and feeding the muck rutted
by hooves and feet,
and with that, the sun hurts my eyes,
and I look for the sparse circles of shade, spread
on the ground in silver dollars, the world
shrinks into a tunnel and someone
gives me water.

I wish our guide
had said that the carcasses
fed Zeus's people

that they were grateful
for his munificence.

Night Sky

You got lost on the way home from rapture.

I called the police
winced when they said
that you had chosen not
to come home.

I gathered your books in a white
nightgown, laid them out in constellations
on the driveway.

The neighbours
watched from plastic chairs, passed
around sandwiches and coffee
on take-out trays.

I am conscious of how I look to them
as I turn in my sky,
an unnamed planet
too far away to take seriously.

Last night

I watched Right whales
on television, mammals mating soft
in hard water churning
the same slow dance for millennia making
a u-turn across the dance floor of the earth
from ocean to earth to ocean
a notion that makes the heart drop and shrinks
quotidian details to mere specks in murky waters

but it was the motion
of their mating
belly to belly
that took the strength out of me
and made me ache.

Paddy Chitty

Kerry

Thank you for your extrodinary kindness & support.

Paddy C.

Do They Call Her Doris Now?

> ***Evelyn Dick was charged with "killing her husband and the strangulation death of her infant son. In the fall of '46, she was sentenced to hang, but lawyer J.J. Robinette was able successfully to appeal the sentence. She was paroled in 1958 with a new identity."***
>
> ***—The Hamilton Spectator, Feb. 28, 2006.***

In the dim café, a caucus of elderly lawyers pick
sweet lamb from the rack of past trials.
An ancient woman sits alone, backlit by blue
lights that hang above the bar.
Rhinestone eyeglasses dominate
her pinched face, accentuate
dark eyes. A carmine lipstick line
links sagging jowls.
It's the Thursday before a long weekend.
The waitress folds white napkins,
asks: *Are you going away, Doris?*
No, says the woman. *Too much to do.*
She pays, picks up her
take-out bag, walks
stooped into the afternoon. A lawyer gapes
out the window, sees the bent woman,
feels déjà vu rattle his bones.

Practicing for the Prom

In Memorial Public School in Hamilton, Ontario, the boys' and girls' gymnasiums were located in the basement on opposite sides of the building. To travel from one to the other without going outside, students cut through a tunnel-like furnace room.

The girls fear-glance back, quick step
through the tunnel. Dim lights shadow-play
on canvas mats that crouch beside stacks
of boxes. A landlocked Hydra
gorges coal, growls, snaps. In the larger gym,
stale air—the scent of boys,
a turn table, 78's where Sinatra waits
with Johnny Ray to take a spin
at centre floor. Dance partners
size each other up like adversaries
in *High Noon*. Needle set to vinyl,
Dean Martin croons *Memories*
are Made of This accompanied by mantras—
1, 2, 3, 4. Hands used to clutching
baseball bats grip partners, bodies
one foot apart. The whites of Margaret's
saddle shoes are scuffed and scarred
by Ben's spring-catalogue rubber
boots. Ernie's eyes grab and fondle
Brenda's breasts. She overlooks
his zigzag part, flecks of dandruff
Brylcreamed down,
thinks how it would feel
                                        to kiss a frog.

Friday Night Frights

Dad's butt obscures the RCA.
He bends at the waist, turns
the dial. A click and a buzz
and the grey screen labours
towards black and white
Friday Night Fights:
the Marquess of Queensbury rules.
Rocky Marciano, Ezzard Charles.
Jimmy Powers calls the punches,
the bell counts the rounds. Clang.

Cut to Gillette's
jingle—*look sharp, feel sharp*
with the quickest, slickest
shave of all. Metal scrapes
against metal
on the ring that glows
in the kitchen, a pop, pop,
promise of corn.

Ringside, Dad in his armchair
bobs and weaves, his head
jerks, cigarette ash
lengthens. Left jab
to the chest
he takes
            the pugilist's blow.

Adjustments

My brother controlled the rabbit ears on our first TV, a Phillips
in a fake wooden box. Left, right, forward, back, and I called out,
no, the other way, that's it, leave it there, no, don't take your hand
away. He bunched a wad of foil or a bent coat hanger
onto a bunny ear. The picture rolled. Flurries to blizzard to wobbly
diagonal bands. The speaker howled like our dog, left alone.
We moved back and forth from chair to set, adjusted the horizontal
or vertical hold. A twist of the dial showed an Indian test pattern
from Buffalo, or peanut-shaped Uncle Chichimus, on the CBC.
One day we found a black and white picture of the house
where we called for Wesley on our way to school. How was this
possible? We had to know. I ran down the block past Woolcott's
Footwear with the x-ray machine you slipped your feet into
and abracadabra saw skeleton feet right through your shoes. Past
the bicycle shop where Dad bought my Schwinn. All the way to Croft's
Radio & TV. Inside their window, a television set and stuff that
made it work, like the camera pointed straight at me. I stared into
its big round eye, waved a *hey look at me* to my brother back home.

It Seemed Normal Then

You on the porch, Smith & Wesson
in hand, we four huddled
inside, warm,
waiting for midnight.

Your breath in white puffs.
Puffs from the barrel. Its greeting,
Pop, Pop, Pop,
Happy New Year!

You returned from a fishing trip with your gun.
I never leave bullets in the chamber,
you said, stowed it,
your hiding place no secret.

Little sister straddles the chesterfield's arm.
I'm a cowgirl. Giddy-up,
Shoot 'em up.
Bang.   Bang.   Bang.

Points at the window,
aims at the bus stop,
aims at the grocery shop,
Bang.   Bang.   Bang.

Mother grabs the gun.
Where did this come from?
Could it be loaded?
Points it at the floor.

B O O M!
Reverberates.
Hole in the hardwood,
Daddy's shop below.

Mother's colour like smoke
from the bore.
Goes to bed.
Saturday shot.

The Dry Cleaner

He ground out his cigarette, entered
the tin-sided plant behind
his shop where loads were sorted
on the counter that ran on one side to the Varsol vat.
He used a shortened hockey stick, forced down
trouser legs and jacket arms
that struggled to surface in the chemical bath.

Load done, rubber gloved,
he trolled the tub like a woman
fishing a wringer washer for wayward
socks. Solvent extracted, clothes tumbled
inside a giant rodent wheel of oak and mesh.
Hodgepodge dislodged
from pants' pockets—the clink of coins,
kerplunk of penknives and packaged condoms.

Cleaned clothes clutched to chest, nostrils seared,
he escaped the umbrella of lethal fumes,
savoured his first deep breath outside.
He wore a path through forty years,
a tick-tock, eight-day clock
wound tight.

The Dry Cleaner's Daughter Goes to the Invisible Mender

Her dad's Oldsmobile idles at Cannon Street's curb.
She jumps out, loose hair whipped-wild, fragrant with *Prell*,
clothing clamped beneath one arm, the other raised to knock.
She dreads the turning knob, the rasp, the reek
of rutabaga and fish within.
Dreads the grey-man mender,
his rumpled trousers and vest, dreads the sea hag, his wife.

He lets her in. She pushes the mending into his arms.
He hunches to the back where he will bend
to the garments, pick threads from hidden hem or seam,
weave, first warp then weft, create invisible mends.
He returns now with last week's work bundled to go.
She flees with the package to the waiting car.
The wind through its windows untangles
the turnip and cod caught
in the fabric of her clothing and hair.

The Fish Monger Next Door

A Piscean air ponged off his canvas apron,
a Picasso rendering in fish gut spray.

Stink painted his store, inside and out.
Stink painted the liquefying remains

of the ice he dumped at the end of the day
by the pink hollyhocks behind his shop.

His smile was inverted. His skin scaly.
Thick-lensed glasses enlarged his eyes.

Compelled by the waters of his id's dark side,
he chased fleeing children with the head of a trout.

The slimy puppet opened and closed its flaccid
mouth; it gloved its doppelganger's hand.

Drinking in 1960's Hamilton

Beer on tap flowed like Albion Falls.
You snapped a cap o' Red Cap. At The Brewer's Retail,
some people wrote Albert Schweitzer or John Lennon
on their purchase order. Pub lounges were two-faced—
men only, and ladies and escorts. In Paddy Green's,
everyone below thirty got carded. Waiters sloshed
froth-crowned amber, hustled trays of stubby
bottles, stout-topped glasses through a grey haze.
Thumped them down on round tables. Like an endless
loop of shooting gallery ducks, filled, plonked
gathered until lust call drinks were drunk.
Drunks spilled onto the sheets, streets—
what the fuck does it matter—they puked, spattered
everywhere. Riding with a designated driver was less
likely than a stroll on the moon
for the spewing green gargoyle with the car key.

Across the Bay toward Paradise
January 3, 1928

A colony of residential boathouses once stood at the western end of Burlington Bay (Hamilton Harbour) and on the shoreline of the Dundas Marsh (Cootes Paradise), in Hamilton, Ontario.

Had someone looked across the ice from the boathouse colony
in Cootes Paradise and Burlington Bay that first workday
of the year, they would have seen a speck barely visible
in the east amidst the grey. Not an ice cutter planning a path to float
hewn blocks, but a man taking a short-cut to work—the cemetery,
where he kept the books. The shacks he was headed towards
must have looked like stranded snipe on the western shore.

He came from the beach strip, left behind the lighthouse,
its knowing eye, the Bastule bridge, a gigantic jaw
that yawned, allowed ships into the channel below. Five miles
he slogged over snow ruts, the slabbing air marked
by his breath. He passed the steel plants on the southern
shore, dragon fire licking the sky. Passed the yacht club
and its members' boats, pricey, land-locked, dry.

As I write, I wonder why he walked
in temperatures so low; his home was modest, not
a shanty, not shunned, as the boathouses were by the city elite
who'd spat their scorn onto the sheets of the Hamilton Herald.
Had he been alone at Christmas? Had the season made him low
on cash, unable to pay the price, the radial line fare?

The boathouse watcher could not have seen him come ashore,
cross the Grand Trunk Railway tracks. Would not have heard
his halting count—the slippery steps to scale the Heights
below Dundurn. Not seen him stop mid-way, or hug an oak,
cheek to bark, as back at home his wife
hung the year's first washing to dry in rigor on the line.

My grandfather was found that day in his office,
cold, slumped at his desk,
stiff as the stilts that moored the boathouse shacks.

Kimberley Dawn

Where to Meet Men

Baptist, Catholic, United,
collectives and trendy shops,
stroller-pushing texters and kale–
lovers mingle along Locke Street on my trek
to the 330 steps. Anxiety driven,
I keep coming back for an unmatched
view if the city, the Bay and beyond.
Plenty of rare warmth on this January weekend.
Only three days ago, the steel
railings that shine in the afternoon light that pours
over the escarpment would have been tongue-tearing.
Today, one last pile of melting grey
at the base attracts mittenless children.
Logo t-shirted climbers with spring
fever pass up and down. A dog-walker
stretches and recounts his hearty
lunch at the pub and the local brew
he's burning off, says "he'll see me around". Mr. Smiley
with his dare to "do one more set" and a gift of bottled
water to motivate me. Chatty Handsome at the top,
who found one of my poems in a crevice last week and saved it:
"Something about a *January Muse.*"

I want to taste the devil,

savour his bouquet, roll over
my tongue his passionate parables,
his blistering imagery. Learn to make
a stock of simmering syllables,
sop it up with crusty loaves.
Find out just what's in that soup
he serves: crimson spices, gnawed bones, sin.
Unearth all the saints who've stirred it before.
Wear my pagan apron, peruse his pantry.
I want to sit at his table as the sparks fly upward
for a gluttonous feast with Chagall, David, Goliath
and Mr. Wilde, my envy and lust shadows on the wall.
In the morning, still glowing,
I will go to the garden
to confess. Breathe
in the reddest roses, a lurid,
burning red.

Peach Pie

And these were her vices.
Long flowery dresses, cursing,
too much wine and disagreeing
with her husband. Leaving
windows open in the rain
all night and running
the car off the bottom of the tank.
Willfulness. Stopping by
unannounced. Sky clad sunbathing.
Licking her finger to mend the pastry
edges and hiding
the last piece of peach pie in the pantry.
Brooding. Love bites. Airing her dirty laundry.
Not sorting the light from the dark.

Insomniac Blues

gotta get me some
free-range turkey-drowsy drug
digest into doze

gotta meditate
down-dog contortion mellow
mantra me to calm

gotta fill that tub
still these restless wanderings
pour on into bed

gotta drain my brain
not worry after sundown
make love into yawn-song

gotta sandman now
dream everything is alright
pray for six hours straight
hope for five tonight

On Sundays

Meditative laps at Victoria Park a part
of my liturgy. On this clouded day
I am hoping
others shy away from a swim.
Instead there's a crowd around my lane
and a bearded man with two boys
In the shallow end, a baptism
beginning. I wish
I'd worn a more modest swimsuit.
I cover myself with a towel, join the flock
in *Amazing Grace*, Amen along.
The man blesses and hugs
Joshua and his brother into the fold
and I slip into holy water.

Longing

Not wanting to flush me
from my hot-flashed slumbers,
he pisses against the cedars
outside the cottage kitchen window
after his solitary trip for coffee and newspaper
and what small-town gossip
he can gather without getting involved.
His strong neck and shoulders are visible
among the panties on the line between us,
still wet from the roaring
storm last night. He shakes and zips,
unaware that I am
there, with French lace under tired flannel, warming
muffins and slicing fruit and wanting
to taste his salty, summery nape. A teasing
cackle of crow from above surprises
him and he responds with genial comments
I cannot quite make out
but wish were for me.

Deep in New York City

I heard no birdsong,
but the performance
by pedestrian and buttercup taxi
was top-notch and tireless
among lofty buildings and swollen
neighbourhoods of iron-escaped walk-ups.
A cacophony of combustion and brassy
inflection the chorus; siren and horn the refrain.
If there were birds there, they would be neon.
They'd leave their nests at dusk, accelerando skyward past
the looming landscape to crescendo at dawn
above the metropolitan glow and hum.

Faire de Beau Rêve

I am at a train station in Paris. Sharp
edges softened by a lifetime of flight.
Unruffled. Bare
shoulders and a mellow smile help
interpret me. *Lady Marmalade*
discothèques through
my mind, down my thighs,
calf and sandal swirling
a purple paisley skirt. Carried away
to a rose granite coast, bottle of Bordeaux,
tender hands. Whispered promises lift
to laughter when the fifth stair up creaks it's greeting.
Breton lace sways on French windows open
to the bravado of high tide. I am led
to the edge, feather-bed enfolded, candlelight
slipping away with daylight

Wolf Wedding

She finds and egg of broken blue
beneath the widespread beech.
"Can I save this for my children Mama?"
Studies it quietly, then announces,
"There's going to be a wolf-wedding."
Scampering on all fours,
she yips and yowls, collects
dandelion puff confetti, tears
birch bark for the alter, picks a violet bouquet.
Guests gather under the spring boughs:
frogs in a bucket, snails and earthworms,
the entire well-hugged wolf clan,
one beloved white cat.
She calls out prayers
for the alpha and wife to love and protect.
The couple share a sip of brook water from the blue chalice.

Years later, between *Charlotte's Web* and *Gone with the Wind*,
a small box with the faded warning: *robin's egg*
do not tuch

Adrift

slipping into the deep
gilt lake
no timeline
  no husband
    no lover
alone between
sun and moon
and dragonfly-hover
immersed in the silence
that soothes the edge
of August

Birgit Elston

For Kerry,

Thank you so much
for everything you've
done for our group

B. Elston

I Recognize November

Copenhagen 2008

My city, built on water, tastes of salt.

Indigo nightfall drizzles the road from the airport.
Beech trees, and oak, slick-naked limbs wet

in the yellow hum of street lights, stretch
towards the shortest day.

Four o'clock dusk, the darkening hour's
candlelight haloes collect the day's events

bring me home.

My mother in quiet rooms, fetching
eiderdown quilts
whispers promises of snow in the morning.

Those muffled black dawns, the fathers
entrenched behind papers, whizzing by in lit-up trains

—and us kids walking to school in the sheltering dark
towards the glow of faraway windows.

1962

My mother fixed lipstick
on her happy mouth, blotted coral-red

before the small mirror
above the kitchen sink.

That day
there was a new coat from my father

one of those stylish garments that women wore
at the time; tapered at the shoulders

the fabric fanning out like a giant lampshade
or a fancy many-tiered cake.

I had to get it, my father said

and the splendour
of this reckless impulse shone from him

to my mother, her face soft, her skin velvet
against the fur collar.

It's much too fine, she said, meaning for her
ordinary, middling life.

. . . And She Danced Away

The threshold
between daylight and darkness, still light-
hearted
          May I have this dance? she joked

and curtsied to an old broom.
          And she waltzed through the scent of night-
blooming jasmine and moon flower vines

her skirt a billow of crimson, a flicker
of gold and that broom in her arms, obeying
her every fancy

but her unruly eyes darted
and dove
          and scanned the dusking sky.

          Remember the night your mother danced?
my father would sometimes say.

But that was much later.

My Father Should Have Been Here

He should have been here
in the front pew with the two of us

my sister, pinned
by the heirloom brooch of gold
and me   in my mother's pearls

spreading to cover
the empty seat between us

while he, unyielding, still
at the house
hair shirt on his back

straight-back chair a rod
for his wretched resolve   not to face

the coffin with my mother inside it
and the two of us gravely sitting.

Ragnarok

In Norse mythology the wolf Fenrir is feared
by the gods for his monstrous strength

The night. The hour of the wolf

when Fenrir, free of shackles, ready
for battle
tears at your sleep
shakes your infinite
                    powerlessness
between his teeth

and Fate, the enigma, summons you
to the edge where your mother
danced   attendance, you saw her fall
the echo of her
bright, red dress forever smaller

and you
gingerly
cup hold of the shell
that shelters
your held breath

that a crack will not hex
the morning

that the wolf will not smell the blood
of naked birds, trembling

before daylight refracts through the shades,
opens that first yielding walk in wet grass

the cool, white dew nipping at your feet.

And Then the Rain

The end of summer
through his open bedroom window

the thinning sounds
of people and cars taking leave

the loon, the mist, the early morning light
combing the still air

drops of vapour
gliding along the washing line   and then the rain

and the dock strewn with yesterday's
swimsuits and towels

the grandchildren's beach balls still outside
and the pails and the small shovels, brilliant colours
paling.

And the old man cannot fathom
how he got here, to this point

where the days of getting up at four a.m.
for work

and Friday's gravel road drive to the lake, payday's
brown envelope folded in his back pocket

the contents later counted and divided
on the mustard-coloured oilcloth

were so long ago
                                        as if in someone else's life.

Outside the Warm Houses

Oblique in the light from the street-lamps
snowflakes fall away in the dark, evening melts
on my tongue.

I'm a thief, I steal
scenes from someone else's life
        a flicker of possibilities where drapes don't quite
reach

where a door opens
to draw a fleeting quadrangle of light in blue snow

where the end of a day rings soft, a woman calls out
time for supper

            the echo of a barely remembered voice
that blew warm against the chill.

First Light

> *The cold Siberian winter produces the so-called "whisper of the stars." As you breathe out, water vapour turns into tiny icicles that fall down with a melodic tinkle.*

over snow, I daydream I'm in Omsk
or Krasnoyarsk or maybe further east, near Irkutsk.

And there's a woman
bunched in capacious sweaters, colourful
kerchief visible under her fur hat, the kerchief crucial

to my image of this woman
who, like me, slogs through snow and morning
light and sweet shadows

our hands in unwieldy gloves, clutching
a pail with bird food.   And were I truly in Siberia

this could be May, or June, and still the blue snow
the pale, frail sun, and the fish
delighting in the silver-striped water of the Baikal Lake

and the ice in the Lena breaking
to make space for sticks and pebbles and waterlogged
leaves, floating icicle tinkles to the Arctic Sea.

And the woman
                    would take off her hat and her woolly vest
and smile a small gladness
                              at the promise of cloudberries.

At the Traffic Light
by the Old Folks' Home

Tonight, we wait

long enough for me to peek, to see
the old people watching TV in their blue rooms

long enough for lamplight to diffuse
into the darkening space outside
and erase the outlines of the day.

If I end up there, my husband says—and it jolts me
that in his voice I detect an amount of acceptance
of what may not be avoided—if
I had to go there, he says, I'd want a view
of the fields at the back
                                        so I could watch for deer.

And suddenly I can picture him there at the window
in one of those rooms, early riser as ever. Look,
he says to me, can you believe
how beautiful they are   …the deer?

Leaving Helsinki-Vantaa

I want to be the girl in the leather hiking boots
with the grey and white rag-socks

that fit so casually
around her legs, her long, smooth, tanned legs

as she gets off the bus ahead of me   outside
an airport-hotel in Helsinki.

A one night chance
layover

en route from Toronto to Copenhagen
stepping outside my life, I want to be her

... with the boyfriend and the matching
rucksacks, and the worn khaki shorts
and the beaded bracelets from some bazaar
in Marrakech.   I ache

at the way her hair
brushes his shoulder, the way she leans into him
how his hand touches her arm, the thought

of the gratifying weight of the rucksack filling up
with careless summer
adventures that are not mine.
And I'll bet they have wine

in those rucksacks, and maps
to spread out, to pore over, tonight   on the hotel bed

in this blurred, sweet delusion
of other options.

Laura Gillis

Dear Kerry,

Thank-you so much for your help & support!

It was lovely to meet you,

Laura

Night Skiing

We should all go, take a trip
next summer, I tell them. Go to a real
Montana ranch where we can
fly fish and ride horses.

I've always wanted to wear
thigh-high fly fishing boots, just the way
I've always wanted to
smoke like Lauren Bacall.

After four Black Russians and a glass of red wine
a man from the city looks up and down
my body and says thigh-high boots, eh?
Well, I'd go for **that**,
and everyone laughs.

My husband makes his way
from the other side
of the room, sits between us in a space
big enough for only half of him.

The boys come in from night skiing
all limbs and barely-beginning moustaches
and smelly boots and cracked voices,
and mothers yell for showers.

And the father who looked at my legs
goes to the kitchen and stands beside his wife,
puts his hand on her back
as she watches the water slowly drain away.

To Be Good

I know it means to have the bank statements
stapled and in order
from month to month so my husband
does not have to lug the giant
A&P grocery bag full of papers to the office
to sort through telephone bills
and restaurant expenses every April
before tax time.

It means to put away the laundry that lies
in haphazard piles around the house
instead of making a fresh pot of coffee
and moving the couch closer to the window
to read Wordsworth and sleep.

It means to volunteer at the hockey tournament,
fill the hospitality suite at the Holiday Inn
that smells of stale smoke
with slabs of pizza and cans of Mountain Dew.

I'm sure it doesn't mean to stand at the stop light
and watch the Greyhound bus
as it moves through town,
and to wonder whether
the seats at the back
are soft, so you can sleep.

What do you bring to the table?
(and other interview questions)

Well, I have a paperweight
that my mother bought me at a flea market.
Swirls of royal blue
encased in clear glass.

And a button collection
in a small dented tin.
My favourite, tiny and cream-coloured
with yellow and red ridges.

In five years? Maybe a cabin up north
where I can wear big sweaters and take
the canoe out in late September on a lake that
looks like the blended browns and reds
of an A.Y Jackson painting.

I can't say why you should hire me.
I can't balance budgets and
I lose things.

But I could sit and have coffee with the woman
I just saw in the waiting room
as she emptied the small garbage pail
into the larger bag on her cart.
Maybe ask her where she's from,
and if she has kids.

Buffet

i.

At the buffet today they served
all you can eat crab legs,
severed red tentacles
sharp and painful to crack.

The Eaters circled stations of food:
bright orange chicken balls,
mounds of slippery pink shrimp,
triangle towers of chocolate cream puffs.

ii

When I was ten I sat at
my uncle's table on Passover
quiet and expectant
as we opened the door
to ask the prophet Elijah to come to us
in the early evening.

My aunt made noodles
steaming from the oven
sweet with raisins and cinnamon,

my uncle served bitter herbs
to remind us
of the suffering.

We ate slowly and in silence
in the warm dining room
with flickering candles.
My aunt cried quietly beside me
then leaned over and smiled,
wiped a strand of hair from my eyes.

The Day

The day she came home from the hairdresser
with her feathery beehive hairdo
and bright red Life Saver suckers,
I threw my arms around her waist
and buried my head in the yellow cotton sundress,
the pillow softness of her middle.
And my mother, who wore berets and
brown corduroy pant suits
and looked like Kim Novak,
bent down and asked if I'd been crying.
She said, *I told you I'd be right back*,
and she put on her apron to make dinner
without even taking off her strappy gold sandals.
I wish you wouldn't worry every time I go out.

A year before, my father and I at the kitchen table.
He fell forward in his chair. His thick, black
glasses hit the Formica table, knocked
over his favourite Niagara Falls mug.
I ran up the stairs to wake my mother,
scared her out of sleep.
Her flimsy baby doll pyjamas
touched my arm as she ran past me.

The spilt coffee.
The sirens.
All that running.

Remember

Today I went to an eco green café
with high ceilings and swanky lights.
The server had dark hair and unnaturally white teeth,
swung his hips as he waltzed by the tables,
leaning in so earnestly to ask if I liked
the sweet potato and apple soup.

I wondered how it was that I was here
in this sleepy, affluent suburb
surrounded by big box stores,
mousy hair pulled back in a ponytail
and an extra few pounds around my middle,
staring out onto the rainy parking lot.

Who is this woman
who drove herself to the emergency room
three nights ago, convinced by an internet site
that a heart attack was imminent?

Embarrassed in mismatched socks
and running shoes stained by
grass cuttings, led through the dimly lit hallway by a
nurse in daffodil-yellow pants,
and hooked up to monitors
beside a ninety year old
who snored and moaned through the night.

> Remember when you were sixteen.
> When you worked up north for the summer.
> How you swam at midnight,
> squeezed the water from your long hair
> and hugged your thin arms around yourself.

A boy with tousled hair and a shy smile
wrapped a Hudson's Bay blanket around your shoulders
and pulled you close.
You stayed up all night smoking cigarettes
and drinking cheap wine

then slipped into the front seat
of his car, turned on the radio
and fell asleep, your cheek
pressed against the window.

Kind of Day

It's a stay in bed
make grilled cheese for dinner
kind of day.
You wouldn't worry about hurting my feelings
or being careful with me today.
I have ugly things going on.

Envy over the better writers,
annoyed with my good friend
over her millions for retirement.
I'm so lucky I don't have to worry about money, she says.

Brenda Ueland said just write.
Don't focus on spelling, grammar, punctuation, better words,
just tell us something real.

Today silence is real.
Don't you ever want to take your fingers
and squeeze the lips of some people,
a light squeeze, not to hurt them
just to remind them.

But this is a dark day
an over the top, forgive me,

but a Heathcliff howling Catherine's name on the moors

kind of day.

Leonard Cohen Says

> *there's not much you can do with anguish*
> *other than write it.*

I'm jealous of the gifts
his anguish gives him.
I want to sit with it a while
but I have an office meeting
and cupcakes to decorate for the bake
sale at my daughter's school,
and the opposite of anguish
shares my bed
and prefers me to
"look on the bright side."

Leonard Cohen's darkness
has a clear pull.
It reminds me that truth
is not optional.

I think about my low
days spent inside,
days my husband can't
get to work fast enough
in his pressed white shirt
and Ken Doll hair,
smelling so fresh and so hopeful.

What is there to do, really,
but put on a pot of coffee
pull my hair back
turn off the phone

dig in.

My Neighbour

My neighbour died a quick death.
His first son was delegated the task
of summing up seventy years
in a eulogy heavy on chronological detail.

The well meaning minister
had us sit and stand,
talked of mercy and resurrection
and mispronounced my neighbour's name.

I waited for the moment
that leaves you knowing something
and if not knowing
at least feeling pulled in,
but it never came.

After the funeral
I went for lunch at a local diner.
The homemade cabbage soup was rich
and warm and filling
and the room was alive
with clanging cutlery and conversation.

My neighbour's wife was in the garden yesterday
pulling weeds and clearing leaves.
She's lost weight and visitors still drop by
but she carries her experience
with something other than grief.

There's an urgency to the piano playing
that I hear through her open window
and in how she walks every evening
in her bright red coat,

as if she's trying to catch up
to herself
the way she imagined she could be
all those years ago.

The Dying

After a day spent with the dying
I want to buy cigarettes and smoke
them in the parking lot
overlooking the city.
Then I want to sleep.

The dying make me want to
pack my red suitcase,
a Value Village throwaway,
and get in my car and go.

After a day with the dying
I went to a party where my husband
tended bar for a local charity.
He wore a kilt and pulled up his
dress pants and danced behind the bar.
People said *it must be nice*
living with someone so happy.

My husband doesn't worry
about the dying
because he has God.
He'll say, *oh that's too bad,*
but he'll still enjoy his dinner.

I told a colleague at the party
about the dying and he said
good for them
and talked about their spirit
and the positive energy
they leave behind,
but he was slurring and
looking down my top.

I don't know how much room to leave
for the dying.
If you took a day to sleep for each,
you'd be asleep all day every day.

You'd be one of the dying.

Sandra Lloyd

Cannot thank you enough. You're the best!

Sandy

The Old Furrier's Vault in the Village, Now a Salon

Few people know about the vault
or the man named Frank who lives within,

its door so thick and heavy
he fixes it open with a chain—

the only entrance to his one-bulbed home
with walls he painted flat black.

He'd be trapped for life
if the door snicked closed.

Certainly none of the patrons
who come to be refreshed know,

the women who tell secrets to their stylists.
My own stylist says she plans to write a book

about all she hears, which makes me
closed. She confides in me, instead.

It's how I learn of Frank,
who cooks on a hotplate in his vault

uses the patrons' washroom
for his own needs, the rare person

who keeps to himself.

Displacement in Westdale Village

On Dromore Crescent a huge magnolia grew,
soft pink hands celebrated until
fallen fingers became nuisance—
sweeping work for a man who worried
someone would slip and fall on the petals

while nearby maples reseeded, hurling potential trees
on veined wings, adding to the mess
another neighbour raked
later, cursing the maple seedlings
he'd have to cull

near an aging cherry tree that lost a large branch
after flowering efforts.
The cherry tree's owner cried,
We bought this house because of that tree!
to which a city worker responded
in the flat tone of one called upon
to repeat himself:
Trees have lifespans, sir,

while an enraged woman wrapped herself
around an ailing oak to save its life, yet

when a tree nearby fell, almost killing someone,
hundreds of feared trees were felled,
trees over which no one mourned or protested

while the woman clung
to her ancient oak,
insensible.

Through Time

And to think that not so long ago, human life was simple in comparison.

—anonymous quote from an email

After typhus and cholera epidemics we stopped
dumping outhouse pails in the streets. We still died
of diphtheria, diabetes, pertussis, TB, mumps,
measles, polio, a scratch . . .

We lived roughly forty-seven years bound
by circadian patterns, buried babies
and feared milk: *the white peril.*
Doctors stopped by homes

but we couldn't telephone.
Illness bankrupted.
Travel took ages, rattled bones,
killed children. We managed insanity

with insanity. Air and minds thickened
with smoke, movements were constrained
by mud and doctrine in cities as flammable
as alcohol and temperaments.

We wore felt bowlers, straw boaters, wool homburgs,
trousers cuffed and creased, collars tall and stiff.
In long skirts, sleeves mutton-full, corseted,
our hourglass shapes trudged through muck and manure.

Crawford Lake

Under a blue sky the stainless snow
absorbs everything. Horses
and their unwitting farmer
pull a loaded sleigh across
the meromictic lake's
petrified surface.
With the whip's crack
the ice gives
the horses scream
Farmer Crawford lunges away
from the confusion,
watches his team descend,
writhe down, and down
into the black, out of sunlight's
range, far from oxygen,
in still water
no caress of bacteria
nor tender decay.
The horses lie intact
the lake their stable
coats gleaming
manes flowing
eyes shining
reins ready, should work
be resumed.
Some say under the moon's full light
the horses' eyes glow red.

Surface Tension

Every year someone drowns in Go Home Lake:
a late-winter fisherman on a snowmobile
failing to clear the slushy gap
between ice and shoreline;
or boats, loaded with drunken cottagers, whirring
at high speeds through the Haunted Narrows
hitting deadheads that float quietly
down Flat Rock Falls from upriver;
or the child unsupervised by parents believing
their son has common sense enough
not to slip on damp rocks and be found
face down in the boat house,
blond hair a feathery fan
waving across the murky surface
dotted with tranquil water striders.

Subjunctive Moods

Uhta—the time just before dawn,
the breathing space for wishful thinking
like the time she hid a note in a bread bag
asking a boy to write to her, because words
would have been enough. She left the bag filled
with loaf heels saved for seagulls outside
his door before dawn and cried
all the way home from Florida for the loss
of his long Indiana vowels, reliving the surge
when he took her hand on the beach and asked,
Would you walk with me? And she'd answered,
No, I shouldn't. But perhaps she should have.

Uhta—the breathing space for wishful thinking
when she drove to work with a man in early hours
and the car windshield deflected words
in a way that allowed private thoughts
to come and go. She'd felt him lean
into her talkative hand whenever it found
his arm. His engagement to another
a high fence flaunting graffiti statements
like *thou shalt not* . . . but given the chance
perhaps they would have.

Uhta—the breathing space for wishful thinking
when she and a friend walked their dogs
before sunrise and she said words to him
that humour could not have hidden:
It's a good thing you're moving away,
or we might've had an affair.
He was quick to pose a question:
Would you say that again?
And she said, *No, no I couldn't* . . .

Learning a New Language

I've caught an inflection of sorts,
have started to dream
in Old English.
My professor emails a love note
in our new shared tongue: He says,
For þam þe ic þu lufe,
—because I love you,
the last words in my mind
before waking and I believe
him, although *lufian*
is a weak verb—*to love.* We read
together, riddles filled with double
entendres and I laugh as if understanding
the hard words, rising nuances.
I will never tell him I don't care
about the words, want him
to keep reading because there's something
about his lowness, tales of heroes, endless
glory, the faithful. We consider St. Edmund
spear-stuck with shootings, bristled
like a hedgehog, honourable.
My professor—an accusative,
my direct object, a stripling
prince who wraps my body
in silver and gold, kisses and carries
me to battle and later I lie
like sweet treasure, awakening
to the fact that it's pointless
to be immersed here
in a dead language.

Falling in Love
at Head-Smashed-In Buffalo Jump

He is fifteen, the hunt is over.
He hunches under a lone
tree on the sandstone ridge that divides
the rolling land. Earth skids beneath.
A brown-eyed girl marks
seasons on a terrapin shell.

Grasshoppers zip, a snake
twists. They signal her body
will be his—a series of orbs
and curves giving rise to
a woman where a mere girl was
before the sun dance.

There are layers to this mating
ritual. He pleas for godly
interference, a change
in the winds to be able
to track his need
and overcome.

Commodity

At first I don't see naked people
on St. Maarten beaches,
I see modest bathing suits
on milky lovers, sun-baked friends
copper-toned children, wrinkled wealth
dark poverty, people like apples
pears, cinnamon sticks, holding piña coladas
with umbrellas and pineapple wedges.

Then I see nudity
and her two companions—
men taking turns saying:
Stand on my hands.
They throw her into the air
steal touches as she slip-slides around them
in the see-through sea.

Nudity walks the length of the beach alone
struts, sits, stretches face down
makes breast prints in soft sand
opens legs, closes legs
finger-combs her hair, strokes her skin
sweeps her fingertips in wide arcs in the sand
to exaggerate the breast prints.

She meanders back to the men
past rainbow bathing suits on sneak-a-look
tourists who witness
this part of the exchange
for free.

Patternicity

I'm here to talk to myself,
snoop around silk flowers
and paraffin lights. I resist stealing
an ornament tucked near a grave.
White-tailed deer, two adults and a yearling,
sneak down the narrow road
behind me. They pause when I pause;
we proceed, the four of us.
If these three deer are my dead ones,
what are they here to say?
Elegant ruminants, backlit
by the sun, munching on flowers strewn
over fresh mounds.
Cream-coloured roses hang
from their mouths.

Elizabeth Tessier

Kerry

Thank you so much for being a part of the evening. It was a huge relief. Elizabeth

After Dundurn

i.

The last of two sisters married to two brothers,
she tarries—her arrival all those years ago
with nothing but a trunk of black
clothes, mourning her young husband,
the small hand of her son, curled cold.
The loose dress of grief hid another
son, gone to God just after.
Stripped of all but sister,
she docked in Hamilton.

She was the other Mrs. McNab, a double
bond of blood and law.
And there was blood to catch
in fine handkerchiefs
and her sister's large-eyed daughters
wanting answers
which she gave them
bead by bead, phrase by phrase.
God's naked body and that face
of suffering they would soon know
with their mother's death.

Neither wife nor mother,
she stayed. Mr. and Mrs. McNab,
though they could never marry.

The years wore a dark patch
on the velvet prayer stool.
The first crunch of the gravel came back to her
as she wandered the halls after Sir Allan's death
in the unpacked black of mourning
before the final auction of the contents.
Year by year, cool beads through her fingers,
room to room, reviewing the list
of the things in the house that
she lived in for years
yet was never hers.

ii.

Like her I wander the pine and plaster halls
before I leave, reviewing my life here,
girl to woman in a house not my own.
I dust and sweep the museum with gloved hands
in the last days of a job
that might have been mine, but isn't.

I suppose she had her faith and her health,
as she clutched the ornate rosary
and pushed open the panes now sealed shut.
I have neither, and worry about
my future after Dundurn.
Her future lies in a century-old story,
like a black skin-bound Bible.

Dundurn, its grand façade.
It never was quite what it wanted to be either.
Never quite paid for or finished,
despite the airs it assumed.

Soon to work elsewhere,
I drag my bad leg and gather the garbage
of straggling tourists.
Imagining belonging. Imagining place.

Divorce

I am an immigrant
divided from familiars. Here are
strange birds, temperatures, flowers.
Away from the arid country of my home
the desire to leave turns nostalgic.
But even a ticket back would be no return
and all the same reasons to leave
live there, an irreparable division
of soul,
the sort of division that makes our children
strangers.
Even the sky has changed.
We wrestle with new gods
forever severed from those
we used to serve.
To thrive and feel more inexorably
the lingering guilt of leaving,
the melody of folksong for which one has forgotten
the words. A confusion of foodstuffs,
a feeling of unpaid debt. A cost that
can't be measured in the new currency.
My need to leave leads me to this place,
a country of possibility that demands
strength, bold hope,
that leaves me
anxious, groping my way without
traditional footpaths.
Reckless, I learn to speak myself
in a new vernacular.

Kitchen Witch

Perhaps I should be kinder
to the gingerbread witch
trying to hold it together
with royal icing.

Crazed fairy stepmother
wanting to roof and candy
solid walls and sweet shared excitement.

Not always possible—
the holding together of hope
made of sweet care and egg white anxiety
subject to the gravity of the situation.

Perhaps I should be kinder to myself
in a room full of dirty dishes
when I could have been asleep.
I spent an evening on an architectural task
when I could have
just asked them how their day was.

But every parent has weaknesses,
especially those balanced on steps,
lost in the forest
without stones or breadcrumbs.

Building a home from scratch,
giving candy to children—
it's the only spell I know.

The Bath

My thighs loom, the heat
creates a line
where red skin meets white.
It may be the same water
pumping through
the city's circulatory system,
the same warm holding.

I float amniotic, remembering.

Her large veined legs mapped her past.
The purple around an arterial scar
from a fragment of plate-thrown fury
from her father's hand. Though she told me
something else at the time,
I can remember only the truth
I learned after she died.

I studied her body
the way I studied
the beach or a fallen tree or the cover of a book—
with love.
It comforts me now—as judgment floats up around my
thighs—
to see my body as I saw hers:
a luminous, lighthouse presence.

Tantrum

Her fists strike.
But I sense some measure
in where they land
that comforts me.
You are just tired. I hear myself say it,
remember the sharp
indignant pull I felt on hearing
my mother voice the same.
Realize now she wasn't dismissing
as much as forgiving me.
My daughter's back arches away.
She thrusts her small body
with what seems a thousand pounds pressure.
I barely hold on,
think of what she said to her father
in a princess unicorn voice:
Then there will be pills and treatments and
treatments and pills and Mommy will be all better!

I wonder if this resistance is a pull
away from the helpless burden I will be.
She makes a deal with me,
then breaks it,
tries to bargain a better one.
I know the bargaining impulse well.
Take hold of her straining power
until she goes slack.
She rearranges herself in my lap,
then nuzzles in.

Canning

My mother's long fingers
push small pimpled cucumbers
into narrow-necked Masons.
The steam of hot acid
tingles our nostrils
as she pours the brine
through a wide-mouthed funnel.

Beside her,
jars stand shoulders together
like bridesmaids.
Fruit suspended in syrup.
A white bowl striped
with the skimmed pink
strawberry foam
we ate with a spoon.

Years later, I followed her floral apron V and bow
down the cellar steps
to another era,
surprised by the bark-backed logs
that held the stately papered walls above.
And there, the way dollars hold time,
hours of her life stored up ready
for casual visitors to dinner.
Land of forward planning,
of quiet women boiling up jars
to push through fruitless Februaries.

After my mother's death
I went down
for her poem of peppers
from a late summer of her health.

Now I lid and twist it
with this.

Winging

Winged with her father's lovely hands
my youngest flies
to set the angel on top
from where she lies prone
in a cardboard box from the family
home, recently sold.
She brings the message
of the temporality of home
and the persistence of spirit.

She hovers over the cacophony
of a multitude of hosts—mixed messages,
mixed family, mixed traditions,
the ghosts of Christmas past,
felt and fur of first home,
fragility of first marriages,
voices of Nanas and Aunts
no longer with us.
Our children empty the box
with the enthusiasm of inclusion
for every lost and broken soul.

Our angel flies slightly askew
head to one side as if contemplating
what holds us.
Mismatched tree and half lit menorah
our resistance to any given tradition,
a commitment to what feels true
in our religiously irreligious home,
holding to the mysteries of light and birth
without the usual answers,
winging on desire always
a flight towards.
Homing.

Homecoming

She is lying in your bed, her hair a mess.
Her long finger traces the figure
of your new tattoo,
an anchor splashing through waves
finding ground.

The trees have grown, the bed leans,
no longer an outstretched plain
but a valley.
The top of her foot slides under your great arch
like Hermes' sandal.
You have never been so close to anyone.

You have passed the test,
not mere return but a suitable suitor,
your broad bow bent to her task.
And that was the easy part.

Did you begin with the Ciconians,
the equal measure of loot and wives
interrupted by their allies?
Or did you skip to the Cyclops,
leaving out the milk and cheese
and going for the gore of spattered brains?
Crafty Odysseus, needing most to be known.
Did you share or not share about the beautiful hair?
You mounted the silver throne, you alone.
The wine, the goddesses in leopard prints
like a Versace ad.
You had it all, except
home.

And by home, not your mother in the shadows
or your father, asleep in the orchard,
or even the blood-washed palace,
but this.
Like-mindedness.

Your mother said to tell your wife
that the body and the soul separate
after death.
She meant
this is the only time
our souls can confer
body to body.
Only now can our urgent hearts take hold
of each others' big thighs
and come home.

The Gentleman's Chair

Not manly but gentlemanly
its smoked salmon velvet
and shiny wooden scrolls.
The curving upper slightly reclined,
ball of the seat with low slung arms.
I sit down thinking I'll read,
let myself fall back
onto its quilted curve
and naturally
my hands come to rest
at the end of the arms,
the slightly flattened part of the velvet,
while my fingers gently curve to hold
the wooden hand-holds that are like
the ends of a violin.
The whole experience so sensual
that it's amusing to think of the chair
in the unused parlour of a Canadian home.
The sort of home where such an investment
might be a sign of hard work
and God's obvious favour,
the two inextricably linked, the pink
chosen by a woman as an escape from austerity.
She chose a matched set, his and hers:
her own, lower and without arms,
his with the gentle curves that hold like labia.
We have no parlour or drawing room,
only a room dominated by a computer
and a spare leather couch, so that
this ornament of desire
the colour of arousal
leans back in our bedroom
displaced from its corseted origins.
Instead of tidies and potted palms
it is witness to our raised sleigh bed
and the luxury of lovemaking by electric light.
And when I sit in it, with its low bent legs,
I am the perfect height
to take my gentle man.

May All That's in a Seed

May all that's in a seed be in this day,
Here, as these master gardeners take hands,
That their begin that's planted here today
Grow radical and plumule shoot of bands.

That what is natural and good should grow
Like the ringed outward growth of trees,
The open milkweed pod of love they sow
The diaspore of lichen the wind frees.

Their osprey and deep water wonder give
A nesting pole of meaning to our lives.
The politics of care they teach and live
A watershed from which their love now thrives.

We come together with them on this day
To ride the waves, to dive the pitch and foam
Like a dolphin super-pod at play
Take joy out to oceans of our own.

Notes

Pauline Hewak

"Altar of Hiero" ~ In Syracuse, Sicily, built by the Hiero ll (269-216) in honour of Zeus. One of the largest altars of the ancient world.

"25 Charlton" ~ The address of a medical building in Hamilton, Ontario. In Etruscan and Roman religions, the haruspex divined the will of the gods by examining the entrails of sacrificed animals.

Paddy Chitty

"Dundurn" ~ Dundurn Castle, a Tuscan villa style mansion completed in 1835, was built by Sir Allan Napier MacNab, a former Premier of the United Province of Canada (Canada West, formerly Upper Canada—present day Ontario, and Canada East, formerly Lower Canada—present day Quebec) from 1854 to 1856. The mansion stands atop Burlington Heights overlooking Burlington Bay in Hamilton, Ontario.

Birgit Elston

"Ragnarok" ~ In Norse Mythology, the final battle between the gods and Evil, when the wolf Fenrir breaks free of his magic chains and brings about the destruction of the world. It is predicted that a new, perfect world will rise after the devastation.

Sandra Lloyd

"Crawford Lake" ~ *meromictic lake* – a lake in which the layers of water do not mix or circulate thereby creating a unique set of stable conditions, including anoxia and cold temperatures which serve to slow the rate of decomposition.

"Learning a New Language" ~ For þam þe ic þu lufe—from the Old English or Anglo-Saxon language meaning 'because I love you'; lufian: the Anglo-Saxon verb 'to love'

"Subjunctive Moods" ~ uhta – the Anglo-Saxon word meaning the period just before dawn

"Patternicity" ~ *patternicity* – the tendency to find meaningful patterns in meaningless noise

Elizabeth Tessier

"Tantrum" ~ In Greek mythology, Ananke, was the personification of destiny, necessity and fate. She was the most powerful dictator of fate and circumstance. Mortals, as well as the Gods, respected her and paid homage. According to the ancient Greek traveller Pausanias, there was a temple in ancient Corinth where the goddesses Ananke and Bia (meaning violence or violent haste) were worshipped together in the same shrine.

Acknowledgements

We would like to thank the editors of the following publications where several of these poems have appeared. Sandra Lloyd: *Other Voices; Hart House Review; University of Toronto Magazine, iPad version; PRISM International;*Birgit Elston: *The Saving Banister; The Bridport Prize; The Elora Writer's Festival Website;* Kimberley Dawn: *Quills.*

Special and continued thanks to Marilyn Gear Pilling, our mentor, editor and friend, for her excellent instruction, her generosity and her support. This book would not have been possible without her. We appreciate her patience and wisdom throughout the editing process.

Heartfelt thanks to Richard Grove (Tai) and Hidden Brook Press for this opportunity.

The editor thanks Paddy Chitty and Sandra Lloyd for applying their technical and proof reading skills on the last lap. She thanks all seven poets for enriching her writing life, that is to say her life. E.B. White said, in **Charlotte's Web:** *It is not often that someone comes along who is a true friend and a good writer.* To have seven come along is my kind of miracle.

CPSIA information can be obtained at www.ICGtesting.com
Printed in the USA
LVOW13s0306090514

385027LV00003B/15/P

9 781927 725